Building Your Business
by Faith

Growth Strategies for Business Success

Shiketa Morgan

First Printing, 2019

ISBN 9781690652953

Printed in the United States of America

Dedication

This book is dedicated to every family member and friend that Cheered for my business growth and supported me as I stepped out on faith to grow my business.

I also want to give a special thank you to my husband for being my faith partner. He has truly encouraged me to not give up.

Thank you to my children for helping with the business and sharing their mom with others. I am truly grateful for my dedicated and faithful staff.

My parents have truly been a support on my business growth journey, and I am thankful to have such supporting and loving parents.

My circle of friends and prayer partners has also helped to keep me encouraged and I am most grateful for everyone that played a role in my business growth Journey.

Table of Contents

Introduction

"One can choose to go back toward

safety or forward toward growth."

I believe that you purchased a copy of this book because you desire to Grow your Business. In addition to having a desire to grow your business, I also believe that you have a desire to go to another level in business.

When I opened my first Child Care Center in 2003, I had a vision to own multiple locations. In fact, I carried that vision for eleven years and while waiting for the vision to become a reality, that first location taught me how to manage multiple locations.

Furthermore, while I prepared for multiple locations, I went through 11 years of trials and tribulations and I looked for other buildings as God was preparing me for the business growth that was ahead of me.

Moreover, I can remember looking for buildings and going to banks applying for loans so that I can open a second location and for 11 years, I was running into lots of closed doors.

Today, I thank God for those closed doors, because those closed doors, were not what God had in store for me.

In fact, I have discovered that when you run into closed doors, that is God's way of saying, ***"That's not for you!"***

After 11 years of being in my first Child Care Center, the business began to decline. In fact, I began to wonder what was going on.

I was a faithful tither, I was marketing the business, we had a quality childcare program, however, we didn't have very many children enrolled.

In August 2014, a friend of mine, texted me and told me about a building that was vacant and for lease.

So, I decided to stop by the building. When I pulled up to the building, I knew in my spirit that was my dream location.

After pulling up on the parking lot and getting out of my car, I walked up to the front door and I laid hands on the door; then I decreed and declared this: ***This building will be the next home of Learning Days.***

Making a declaration over the building, activated my Faith, however I had one problem! *I didn't have the money, all I had was **Big Faith.***

In this book, I will share with you, how my Faith in God empowered me to Grow my Business, How to get through hard times by faith, The importance of

Growing as a leader, How to encourage your team to grow and I will share strategies that I used to manage two locations. Moreover, I will share how following the dream in your heart will move you out of your comfort zone.

If you are truly ready to Grow your Business, this book is for you and I believe that after reading this book, you will be inspired and empowered to build the business of your Dreams….***by Faith!!***

> ***Faith Thought***
> *Practice Confidence and Faith*
> *and Your Fears and insecurities*
> *will soon have no*
> *power over you.*
> *~ Norman Vincent Peale*

Building Your Faith for Business Growth

"Your Business will only rise to the Level of your Faith"

The bible defines faith as: "the substance of things hoped for, the evidence of things not seen." So, please allow me to ask you a question: What is it that you hope for that you have not seen yet? Take some time to write down your answer and believe God for it.

____

____

____

____

____

____

____

____

Your Faith is also developed when you hear the word of God and when you trust and believe that what you want will soon become a reality.

Furthermore, we all given a measure of Faith and it is your Faith that will empower you to Grow your Business.

Therefore, I believe that your Business is only as Big as your Faith!

When my Child Care Business was in my Home, I had the Faith to operate from my home. However, when I decided to further my education, I developed my Faith to move the business out of my home. Furthermore, as you can see; increasing your knowledge helps to build your faith.

After increasing my knowledge, along with finding the courage to step out on Faith, I moved into my first Child Care Center in 2003.

In 2003, I had no leadership training, however, I had lots of experience caring for children along with the Faith to believe that I can do it!

The first year of operating a Child Care Center was a very challenging year. In fact, I had no idea that leading others would be so difficult and again I had to educate my self on how to be an effective leader.

Furthermore, the challenges that I faced as a leader almost caused me to quit, however, my Faith was too strong to quit.

In addition to wanting to quit, I was very stressed, and I was becoming a miserable business owner. Along with feeling stressful, my Faith began to shrink.

At this point, I knew if I wanted to survive in business, I had to get some help. So, I invested in a Business Coach. My Business coach had previously operated a Child Care Center (for 17 years) and she gave me lots of great business advice.

My advice to you: There is no need to learn the hard way, when you can learn from someone that has already been where you are trying to go.

Having a Business Coach increased my confidence and I regained hope that I could build a Successful Child Care Business.

Four years later, I began to think about owning multiple centers and I began to study major chain facilities.

In 2007, I began to look for another building. In fact, I can remember meeting with my license representative to look at a building In St. Peters, Missouri. The building was three times the size of my first center and to be quite honest, I knew that I was not ready to operate a facility that would gross a million dollars a year.

With that million- dollar budget in mind, this is when I was inspired to go back to school to get a degree in

Business. Furthermore, I felt in my spirit that I needed to increase my business knowledge and that was one decision I do not regret. Moreover, going back to school prepared me for the growth that was to come, and it was another way to increase my Faith for business growth.

The Business degree that I earned in 2010, empowered me to do great business and I gained a wealth of marketing knowledge.

Then I Faced Another Challenge

In 2010, my enrollment dropped very low and I began to worry about how I was going to pay my staff. Along with my worries, the staff began to talk about the low enrollment, and I knew that I had to do something, or we would be closing the center.

I purchased a book called, the **Law of Confession** by Dr. Bill Winston. That book changed my mindset about the power of your words and how you have the power to create your reality with your words.

After reading the book Law of Confession, I decided to put my Faith to work and apply the principles in Dr. Winston's book.

My first Child Care Center was licensed for 40 children and at that time, I believe that I had less than 15 children enrolled.

One Saturday morning, I went into the center and I spoke to every chair in the center and made the declaration that every chair shall be filled by a child.

Shortly after making that declaration, my enrollment increased, my Faith increased, and I needed to hire more staff.

That season taught me to speak Faith filled words, because after all, your Business will only rise to the level of your ***Faith!***

Please allow me to share with you three easy ways to build your Faith:

1. Increase your Business Knowledge
2. Speak Faith Filled Words
3. Believe that your words have power, so only speak what you want to see manifest in your Business!

As you can see, it took years for me to build my Faith for Business Growth and to be honest, that was only 10 years of my business Journey. As you continue reading this book, I will share more Faith building tips and strategies with you.

I think you get the message; if you want to do Big Business, you must increase your knowledge, speak to your mountains and Believe!!

Faith Thought

It's time to develop Big Faith;
so that you can do BIG BUSINESS!

What do you plan to do to build Your Faith?

____

____

____

____

____

____

____

____

____

____

____

____

Tithing and Business Growth

*Give, and it shall be given unto you;
good measure, pressed down, and
shaken together, and running over,
shall men give into your bosom. ~
Luke 6:38*

I can remember when I first started tithing from my business Income. In fact, I can remember wondering if tithing will work or not.

So, I began to ask questions about tithing, and I studied the bible on how tithing benefited us.

What does the word of God say about tithing?

Malachi 3:10-11 says: " *Bring ye all the tithes into the storehouse, that there may be meat in mine house and prove me now, here with, saith the Lord of hosts, if I will not open up the windows of heaven, and pour you out a blessing, that there shall not be room enough to receive. And I will rebuke the devour for your sake and he shall not destroy the fruits of your ground.*"

For clarification, the word tithe simply means a tenth of your income. Many business owners' questions whether they should tithe 10% of their net or their gross.

I believe that If you tithe from the net, you are robbing God, because this means that you paid your bills before you gave God what He asked for.

However, when you tithe from your gross income, you can certainly expect more to come back to you, because Malachi 3:10 says that when you bring your "tithes" to the storehouse that God will open up the windows of heaven and pour you out a blessing that you will not have room enough to receive. So, why cheat yourself out of a blessing?

Here is another way of looking at Tithing

Tithing is simply giving God 10% of your business income, so that He can bless the other 90%. After all, if you withhold the tithe, you take the chance of it all being devoured.

In my home, my income was five figures and my tithes were hundreds of dollars per month. After four years of operating my business from my home and moving into a commercial location, my tithes went to thousands of dollars per month.

I can remember back in 2005, when I received a tax bill for $5,000. I ignored the bill and one day a tax collector stopped by the business to collect the taxes.

That was an embarrassing day and I was so scared that I would lose my business if I didn't pay the taxes. I agreed to pay $1200 a month until the taxes were paid. The only problem was this: I didn't really have $1200 per month and I decided to not tithes for several months until the taxes were paid. That was a bad idea.

When I stopped tithing, I noticed that my enrollment began to decline. Once I realized that the enrollment decline was an example of how the enemy will devour your business.

I decided to tithe again, and I asked God to replace everything that I lost during that season.

My enrollment increased, I paid the taxes off and I have not stopped tithing since then.

As I continued to trust God and tithe, my Business moved from a 1600 square foot building into a 6,600 square foot building in 2014. Then in 2016, I purchased a second location and I took on managing two locations.

I hope that you can see through my story that tithing blesses and increases your business and withholding the tithes, opens the door for the enemy to devour what you have built.

If you do not believe in the principle of tithing, I just want to say this to you: Ask God to give you a revelation about tithing and trust that He will.

Where do I give my tithe?

Just in case you are wondering, your tithe belongs to your local church home or to a church where you are spiritually fed and connected.

Your tithe is also tax deductible and it reduces your taxable income and is considered a charitable donation. (see your tax adviser) At the end of each calendar year, your church should give you a contribution statement that indicates how much you have paid in tithes each year.

Please Read Very Carefully. This chapter was not written to cause any condemnation or to convict you, but to lead you to a biblical principle that will result in you being **blessed!**

God Answered my Prayer. While I was writing this book, I asked God to increase my income so that I can eliminate some debt. In fact, I asked God for a Breakthrough in my finances.

That breakthrough came in a unexpectant way and the breakthrough increased the income in my Child Care center by 20%.

When I noticed the increased, I yelled, Oh my God!! My husband said, what's wrong? I said, nothing is wrong, God answered my prayer.

That night I couldn't sleep, because I was so excited. Most of all, I couldn't believe what God had done for my finances.

Please remember this: If God did it for me, He will do it for you. I simply prayed, Father God, I ask that you increase my income, so that all my business and personal expenses are covered every month.

Increase Comes from God!!

Faith Thought
And all the Nations shall call you blessed: for ye shall be a delightsome land, saith the Lord of Hosts. ~ Malachi 3:12

What are your thoughts about Tithing? How has this chapter inspired you?

Thinking Bigger Leads to Growth

"WHEN YOU BELIEVE, YOUR MIND
WILL FIND A WAY TO DO IT."
– David J. Schwartz, The Magic of
Thinking Big

Several times a year I read the book, As a man Thinketh, by James Allen. That book reminds me that I will only rise to the level of my thoughts. Along with that, the book reminds me to be intentional about my thoughts.

"The mind guides our footsteps as we progress along the pathway of life."
-James Allen

Please allow me to ask you a question? Where has your mind led you? Have you been thinking about growing your business, but you procrastinate on the growth because you are comfortable where you are?

I want to challenge you to Think Bigger and cast down thoughts of lack, doubt and thoughts that lead to procrastination.

In fact, I believe that your Business will only grow, when you begin to think Bigger!

As I wrote this book, I reflected on my 20 years of Business experience and my business experience has taught me that when I think small, *I only hinder my business growth.*

However, when I began to think Bigger, *the business grew bigger!*

I can remember when I was getting prepared to expand in 2014. My current rent was only $1934 a month and the rent on the new location was going to start out at $4800 a month and increase to $6,600 per month.
When I saw those number, it scared me. In fact, it gave me some anxiety because I didn't know how fast we could get 99 kids in that building to meet that budget.

In addition to worrying about enrollment building, I thought about how the business went from having four employees to fifteen; and thinking about how the payroll would increase.

As I look back today at how I was thinking about the expansion, my thoughts were in the wrong place. I should have been thinking about How Big our God is and the Fact that if God brought me to the building, God was going to provide what I needed!

So, I shifted my focus and I began to think about the income that would come from the location. As I calculated the income, the expenses began to look smaller to me. God also reassured me in a Dream that we would be ok financially. During that expansion, I had a dream that money was falling out of my pockets and when I woke up, I told my husband, we have nothing to worry about, God is going to bless us with the finances for this building.

That season taught me this: Thinking Bigger takes your mind off the problems and places your mind on what is possible for your Business.

*The biggest obstacle to wealth is fear. People are afraid to **think big**, but if you think small, you'll only achieve small things.*
-T. Harv Eker

If you are ok with your business being small, this book is not for you and you might as well stop reading now. However, if you want to do big Business and keep growing, Keep reading!

I want to challenge you from this day forward to start thinking Bigger and trust God. If you don't know where to start, here are a few ideas:

1. Connect with and follow people who are doing Big Business. I love to follow CEO's of Major corporations.
2. The next time that you buy lunch for your staff, Go Big. Instead of buying deli sandwiches', order some Red Lobster.

3. Ask yourself the following question (s): What will be my next Big Move? What can I do to take my business to another level?
4. Market your Business Big! Is it time for more Facebook ads? Does your social media post reflect that you are Thinking Big?
5. Write down all the Big thoughts that you have for your Business and talk about it with likeminded people.
6. Read books by People that have built Successful businesses.
7. Sign-up for a Business Growth conference and gain new insight and get inspired to think Bigger.

If you think BIG then it's going to be Big.
-Emeril Lagasse

Faith Thought: *Your Business will only move in the direction of your most dominant thought. So, you might as well think Big!*

What Do you plan to do to Think Bigger?

Planning for Business Growth

"Growth doesn't just happen; you must plan for Growth."

One thing that I have learned about Business growth is this: If you don't plan for growth it won't just happen!

In other words, if you fail to plan, you plan to fail.

According to Entrepreneur Magazine, *"If only <u>half of startups</u> survive more than five years and only one-third make it to 10, what's the one thing you could do to ensure your company is sustainable? The answer is to create a growth strategy for your business, of course.*

A growth strategy involves more than simply envisioning long-term success. If you don't have a tangible plan, you're actually losing business -- or you're increasing the chance of losing business to competitors."

So, what does long term success look like for your Business? Have you taken the time to write it down?

I want to challenge you to take the time to think about what long term success could look like for your Business.

One year before I wrote this book, I read the book: ***"Pour your heart it"*** by Howard Schultz (CEO and Chairman of Starbucks).

In fact, as I read the book the following quote inspired me to keep growing: *"Either your business is Growing, or it is dying."*

Please allow me to ask you a question: Is your Business growing or is it dying and what are you going to do about it?

Are you ready to create that Business Growth plan? Do you have any idea of how to create a Business Growth plan?

It is simple. Think about what you really want for your Business and put it on paper. Share it with your spouse, your Business partner and your employees.

When you put your business growth plan in writing, this will activate what you need for the Business growth to come to you.

As I write this book, my Business Growth plans includes me opening a location in Atlanta. My husband and I are currently looking for a building, we travel from Atlanta to St. Louis once a month to check on Our Center in St. Louis. The plan is to have multiple locations and provide families with quality, safe, educational childcare that trains children in the bible.

Once my dream becomes a reality, I'm sure the growth will continue in Atlanta. Moreover, as I grow, I plan to spread the knowledge through my books, podcast, coaching sessions and speaking engagements.

So, what will your growth plan look like? Write it down and watch your dream, become your reality someday!

Growth Thought:

"If you want to build a great enterprise, you have to have the courage to dream great dreams."
~Howard Schultz

Describe your Business Growth Plan?

____

____

____

____

____

____

____

____

____

____

____

____

____

____

____

____

____

Developing a Mindset for
A New Level

A New Level requires a New Mindset

When it comes to business, mindset is everything. In fact, your mindset will determine the level of success that you will attain.

Moreover, I believe that your mindset will either help your business or it will hurt your business; and therefore, it is important that you develop a new mindset for every level that you reach.

In the fall of 2014, my child- care business moved from a 1600 square foot building to a 6,600 square foot building.

Within a week of moving into the building, we were noticing that several children had their fingers smashed in doors.

After an assessment, we realized that the children were not accustomed to having so many restroom doors. In fact, our old location only had 2 restrooms and our new location had 8 restrooms. That was a big adjustment for the staff and the children. So, we had to train the staff on door safety and closely monitor children by the doors.

In other words, we were forced to help our staff develop a new mindset around restroom safety.

Also, we all agreed as a team that the practices that worked at our first location would no longer work at the new location, because our second location was much larger.

So, we had to develop new systems and our management had to develop a new mindset for that new level.

Furthermore, I have been persuaded that the mindset that you start with is not the mindset that will keep you in business.

You must develop a mindset to keep growing and develop new systems or you will be stuck!

In 2016, my husband and I purchased another facility. I met with the staff, developed a management plan, I added the new location address to my business card and my website. Along with updating the marketing materials, I simply began to implement my systems that were already in place at both facilities.

Operating two locations, was very demanding and to be quite honest I was feeling the pressure of going from 10 to 23 employees.

Moreover, it was vital that I had to develop a mindset that could handle managing two locations.

So, I hired two part time secretaries and I began to empower my Center Directors, as I focused on Business Growth.

In addition to making several changes to how I ran the business, I discovered that if I was always working in the business, *I was not running the business, the business was running me; and I went part time.*

If you want to be able to handle more, it is vital that you keep developing a new mindset!

What Steps Do You Need to Take in order to develop a new mindset for a new level?

____

____

____

____

____

____

____

____

____

____

____

____

____

____

____

Growing as a Leader

"Everything rises and Falls on

Leadership"

On August 17, 2017, I published a blog post titled: **Developing the Leader within you will change your business** and I thought I would insert that blog post in this book, because that blog post shares my 12-year Journey of Developing the Leader within me.

"I realized the importance of having great leadership skills when I expanded my home daycare into a center. In fact, my poor leadership skills had a huge impact on my business including; my response to creating change, managing employees, my attitude toward negative employees or even dealing with difficult parents and most of all….my role as the leader in my business.

After I finished typing the paragraph above, I thought, Wow…I was a mess! Yes, I was not ready to expand my business, yet…I was not prepared for all that came with owning a center with 4-6 employees, managing a six-figure salary, conducting business meetings, mentoring employees and so much more that comes along with owning a center.

After experiencing 2-years of having a high turnover rate, hiring the wrong people and having a bad attitude about my business, I was ready to make a change. That change was to Develop the Leader Within me!

Change the Leader…Change the Organization.
~John C. Maxwell

I agree 100% with the John Maxwell Quote above. In fact, reading John Maxwell Books is what changed my business. Reading John Maxwell books, has helped me to discover my strengths as a business owner and inspired me to develop my leadership skills.

Moreover, reading John Maxwell books helped me to discover that the problem was not my employees, it was not the parents, the problem was my attitude about the issues that I was facing.

As I developed my leadership skills, every time that a problem occurred, I reflected on how I could effectively handle it.

I must say that as my leadership skills improved, I was able to restore the unity on my team, my worst employee became my best employee, I developed a supportive relationship with my parents, I trained my employees to be leaders so that they were more effective and the morale in my business improved dramatically.

To be quite honest with you, those changes did not take place over night, however, it did take a period of three years to see some consistency in my leadership and I am still growing as a leader today.
As I write this post, I have 23 employees and I must say that if I had not spent years growing as a leader, I would not be a happy boss lady today.

Now, I take the time to connect with my employees and I value their role in my centers. Furthermore, I believe that if I had not grown as a leader, my business would not have grown into 2 locations with a team of 23."

***I believe that growing as a Leader,
will only Grow your Business!***

What do you plan to do, to grow as a Leader?

____

____

____

____

____

____

____

____

____

____

____

____

____

____

____

____

Letting Go to Grow

*When I let go of what I am, I become
what I might be. When I let go of what
I have, I receive what I need.*

-Tao Te Ching

On October 5, 2018, my husband and I loaded a U-Haul truck and moved to Georgia to work on opening a Child Care Center in Atlanta along with the dream of wanting to live in a new city.

I thought about how we would prepare to move to a new city for almost a year and the hardest part about moving to a new city was leaving my family.

In fact, I realized that I had some real attachment issues as I was preparing to move. My family is my world; however, I knew that if I was going to live out the dreams in my heart, I had to learn to Let Go!

Once we moved to Georgia, I was not used to having so much spare time. I was used to waking up in the morning, going to the Center and being busy all day.

When I moved to Georgia, I was awakened to the fact that I was used to being busy all the time.

Moreover, I had to let go of being busy all the time and develop a more relaxed routine.

Once I learned to let go of being busy all the time, I began to incorporate more personal activities in my day such as:
- Going to the Gym daily
- Having lunch with my husband 3-4 days a week
- Going to Yoga
- Sitting in my back yard and enjoying the beautiful lake behind our home.

I think you get the point, I had to let go of being busy all the time, so that I can develop a more peaceful laidback lifestyle.

Several months after moving to Atlanta, several of my employees that had been with me for at least four years decided to leave. I was devastated because these were employees that I depended on.

I asked one of the employees why she was leaving, and she told me: *"You inspired me to live my dreams and I'm going to my dream job."*

Then I had another employee to leave without any notice and I felt like the business was falling apart.

After seeking wise counsel, I decided to be patient and wait, because those employees were used to working under my leadership directly.

So, I had to let go and allow God to bring new staff into the business. That was a tough season because my staff is like family to me, however, I had to be ok with the changes and move on.

Several months after all those staff changes, the Center Director told me she could no longer handle the center. Then I thought, God is really showing me who is meant to be in the business.

Thank God I had another Director to put in her place and that move was great for the business. The turnover reduced, the parents were happy, and the Director leaving was really what the business needed.

While I was in Atlanta, I had more time to closely monitor my budget and I was clearly able to see how the centers were doing on a financial level.

After taking a closer look at the budget, I discovered that my smaller location was draining the income from the bigger center.

Then, one morning while in my prayer room, the holy spirit inspired me to look at a dead leaf on a plant that was in my prayer room. What I heard in my spirit was this: Just like that dead leaf, you must cut the dead branches off the business for the business to grow.

That is when I decided to end the lease on my smaller center. The smaller center was only making enough money to pay the employees, the rent and the utilities. Most of all, it was best to let it Go!

Our Dog of 16 years. When we moved to Georgia, we took our dog Gollum with us. Gollum was a 16-year old Labrador mixed with Chow. He was a great dog, however, when my husband and I moved, we added another expense of leaving Gollum in a doggie daycare for 10 days a month while we were in St. Louis.

My children suggested that we bring Gollum back to St. Louis. So, we brought Gollum back to St. Louis and we noticed that he began to have bowel movements all over the house.

My daughter just couldn't keep up with him anymore and He began to just lay around the house. Gollum had arthritis in his legs and was in chronic pain. My family began to get concerned with Gollum's health and was afraid that they would come in the home one day and He would be gone to doggy heaven. As a Family we made the decision to take Gollum back to the Humane Society.

Letting my Dog go was a tough decision, however, my children had grown up, had their own children and my husband and I lifestyle was too hectic to care for a dog anymore, because we were living between two states.

As you can see, Letting go is a vital part of the growth process and I must say that it can be uncomfortable, however, *it is a necessary part of the growth process!*

What is it that you need to let go?

____

____

____

____

____

____

____

____

____

____

____

____

____

____

Growth is not in your Comfort Zone

"You will never change your life until you step out of your comfort zone; change begins at the end of your comfort zone."

According to the Wikipedia dictionary, *"The comfort zone is a psychological state in which a person feels familiar, at ease, in control and experiences low anxiety and stress. In the zone a steady level of performance is possible. Bardwick defines the term as "a behavioral state where a person operates in an anxiety-neutral."*

I was so comfortable with my Child Care Business being in my home, however, the business did not grow until I decided to step outside of my comfort zone and move the business to a commercial location.

In fact, I had so many excuses to stay in my comfort zone including; I didn't want employees, I like working by self and I didn't want the overhead and so much more.

Thank God, that I didn't allow the reasons above to stop me from moving forward and growing my business.

Furthermore, I have discovered that when I get comfortable God will inspire me to go to a new level in business.

When I made the decision to move to Atlanta, I was excited and scared at the same time. Moving to a new city was something I had never done before, however, I was ready to explore life outside of my comfort zone.

As I prepared to move to Atlanta, my anxiety levels were very high. In fact, they were so high that my blood pressure was very elevated, but I didn't
Let anxiety stop me from moving forward.

The day that we moved to Atlanta, I had a major panic attack and I was taken to the Emergency room by ambulance. Yes…I was truly out of my comfort zone.

When I arrived at the Emergency room, the doctor told me that I had anxiety which can come with living in a new city.

The doctor prescribed me some medication that made me very sleepy and I went home to relax. To be quite honest with you, I was fearful of being so far away from my family and I began to miss my family.

That season taught me that when you step outside of your comfort zone, it is vital that you have a strong support system.

My support system prayed with me daily and encouraged me to stay in Atlanta and not give in to the Fear and Anxiety.

I must say that I am glad that I stayed. Moving to Atlanta caused me to discover that I was truly an anxious woman. Furthermore, I was forced to trust God even when I am in an unfamiliar place.

I also discovered that I needed to challenge myself more and do more new things.

My best friend lives in Columbus Georgia. Shortly after moving to Georgia, she invited my husband and I to visit her and her fiancé. So, we packed our bags and drove to stay a weekend at their house.

Again, I felt anxious because I was in a new place. Once we began to have fun, I didn't feel the anxiety as much.

On our way back home to Atlanta, Charles and I were trying to get back to highway 85. However, the GPS took us on a back road. Not knowing where we were, triggered more anxiety and some heart palpitations.

While on that backroad, I could tell that my husband began to get uncomfortable because we had no cell phone reception for about 10-miles; that was one scary road trip.

As I look back on that day, I think about how once I began to relax and I trusted that God would lead us where we needed to go; peace began to fill my heart.

Being outside of your comfort zone will sometimes lead you to scary places and unfamiliar places. However, when you remember that God is with you, peace will over- take you and anxieties will melt.

Growth truly happens outside of your comfort. In fact, if you are not willing to be uncomfortable for a little while, you just may be in your comfort zone for the rest of your life.

St. Louis is my comfort zone, because that's where I was born and raised. I know St. Louis like the back of my hand, and I feel safe there.

Atlanta is outside of my comfort zone. It's a new place and so much to explore. As I write this Chapter I have been living in Atlanta for 10 months now and I have been enjoying looking for childcare buildings. I have met some great people, I love all the great restaurants, I live in a great community and I am looking forward to the rest of my life being the best of my life. Most of all, moving outside of my comfort zone birthed this book.

Furthermore, I have also discovered that I can effectively manage my Child Care Business from another state. Moreover, I can trust someone else to run my business under my leadership. I can have a great life in a city other than St. Louis and I love my new Church home where my pastor is Bishop Dale Bronner of Word of Faith Cathedral.

As you can see, I went through some discomfort, however, it was only temporary, but God had something great for me on the other side of my comfort zone. New doors were opened, A New book was written, and I have been awakened to a new way of living.

You may already be outside of your comfort zone and I hope that my journey has inspired you to keep challenging yourself to go to new levels.

Are you working on stepping outside of your comfort zone in order to grow your business? If so, just remember that you can do it with God's help.

> ***Growth does not happen,***
> ***until you are uncomfortable!***

Please allow me to ask you a question. Are you comfortable today? What is it that you think will cause you to stretch yourself? **If so, describe below.**

____

____

____

____

____

____

____

____

____

____

____

____

Write the Vision and Wait For it

"Write the vision and make it plain."
~Habakuk 2:2

In this chapter my goal is to encourage you to become a visionary leader. In fact, I have discovered that a leader with a vision is a driven and motivated leader.

Furthermore, a leader without a vision is all over the place and goes around the same mountains on a regular basis.

Do you have a Vision for your Business? If so, have you written down your vision? Have you shared your vision with your employees or your family?

When you share your vision with your staff, it helps them to see the big picture and they can see the direction that the business is moving into.

In addition to that, it is vital that you write down your vision because when you write down your vision, that makes it a declaration or a proclamation.

"Your vision is the promise of what you shall one day be; your ideal is the prophecy of what you shall at last unveil. – James Allen

Also, once you write down your vision, read it aloud, because your words have the power to create what you speak!

Moreover, now that you have written down your vision, you must trust that your vision is for an appointed time, but at the end, it shall speak. So, wait for the vision to manifest.

In 2007, I had a desire to operate multiple childcare locations. Then, in 2016, that vision became a reality. It took 9 years because God had to prepare me for what it took to operate two childcare centers.

I must say, it is truly a blessing to see your Vision become a reality.

Today, I am waiting for my Vision of having a center in Atlanta to become a reality. One day before writing this chapter, I was starting to feel impatient, because we had not found a building yet.

So, I talk to a friend of mine about how I was feeling, and she shared a story with me about a Church that got impatient and moved into a building that contained asbestos.

Immediately, my mindset shifted to patience mode and my prayer is now: ***God I will wait on you!***

Here are 7 easy ways to become a visionary leader and to keep your focus on your Vision:

1. Create a vision board. The mind needs pictures and the vision board is a great way to hold you accountable for reaching your goals.
2. Your goals should be related to your Vision for your Business.
3. Do something everyday that will move you in the Direction of your Dream.
4. Be sure that your staff members are for your Vision and Not against it.
5. Keep a Vision Journal and journal about your business progress.
6. Connect with people that are doing what you would like to do someday.
7. Read books by Visionary Business Leaders!

Remember this: If you stay focused on your Vision, nothing can stop you; *but a lack of Focus!*

"Where there is no Vision, the people Perish."
-Proverbs 29:18

Write your Vision....

____

____

____

____

____

____

____

____

____

____

____

____

____

____

____

____

____

____

____

____

Arise and Build

While I was working on writing this book, I am searching for a childcare building in Atlanta. One evening while in my prayer room, I asked God to show me what it is that I needed to be reading in the bible and I heard: ***The book of Nehemiah***.

I knew it was the holy spirit because I had never read the book of Nehemiah before and all that I knew about the book of Nehemiah was that it was a book about leadership.

When I turned to the book of Nehemiah, I discovered that the Book of Nehemiah was about a contemporary of Ezra and cupbearer to the King in Persian palace. Nehemiah's concern for the welfare of Jerusalem prompted Nehemiah to challenge his country men to arise and rebuild the shattered wall of Jerusalem. During the time that the wall was built, there was opposition and abuse within. Despite the struggles that task was completed in only 52 days.

On the other hand, it took years of Nehemiah's life to revive and reform the people of God within the rebuilt walls.

After reading what the book of Nehemiah was about, I can clearly see that God wanted me focused on

Building my Business, so I took some time to study the book of Nehemiah and I took away a few key principles for Building a Business and I want to share them with you today.

1. As you build your business, ask God to strengthen your hands for this good work. (Nehemiah 2:18)
2. The God of Heaven will prosper you; therefore, we his servants will Arise and Build. (Nehemiah 2:20)
3. As you build, sanctify your business. In other words, base your business on the biblical principles and set it apart from anything that is not of God. (Nehemiah 3:1)
4. Make your prayer unto our God and set a watch day and night over your prayers. (Nehemiah 4:9) It is vital that you pray, because this is how you invite God's will into your Business.
5. When you feel weak or afraid while on the Journey of Building, say *O' God strengthen my Hand. (Nehemiah 6:9)*
6. In the event you start to feel weary on the Journey confess, The Joy of the Lord is my strength. (Nehemiah 8:10)
7. God has a great chamber prepared for you (Which is the result of tithes and offerings), and it will lead to new wine and oil.

As you build your business, there are some key things that you must do to help you to stay strengthened and encouraged on the Journey including:

- Prayer
- Speaking the word of God
- Tithing.

Are you ready **to Arise and Build?**

> *Nehemiah said, "Go and enjoy choice food and sweet drinks, and send some to those who have nothing prepared. This day is holy to our Lord. Do not grieve, for the joy of the LORD is your strength."*
>
> *~Nehemiah 8:10*

Are you inspired to Arise and Build?

Are you inspired to Arise and Build?

As You Grow, Take Care of Your Body

I pray **that you** *may enjoy* **good health**
*and that all may go well with you, even as
your soul is getting along well. -3 John 1:2*

I have been building businesses for over 20 years now and I have discovered that building a business can be very demanding on your body.

In fact, if you are not careful you will find yourself working long hours and failing to take care of your body.

As I was writing this book, I began to look back at photos that I took in 2017-2018 and I noticed that I had gained a lot of weight during that time.

I knew that the weight was mostly from all the dining out and from not exercising due to back pain.

In 2017, I was diagnosed with arthritis in my lower back and high blood pressure. That was devastating news, because the arthritis was affecting how long I could sit or stand, and I was forced to work part time at my childcare center.

I believe the weight gain came from me laying around trying to keep the pressure off my back, which caused my blood pressure to increase.

I began to pray about my health, and I was also under a chiropractor's care.

During that time, my staff took great care of the business and they were begging me to stay home and get well.

Then when I moved to Atlanta, I made the decision to take some time to focus on my health.

In fact, I have found that what we deal with in our bodies is a direct result of what we decide to eat daily.

Within two weeks of moving to Atlanta, my husband and I signed up for a gym membership at Gold's Gym. Along with going to the gym 3-4 days a week, we began eating more veggies, we spend more time outdoors and stopped buying sweets for the house.

Several months after moving to Atlanta, I lost over 25 pounds. Within 6 months of moving to Georgia, I went from a size 14 to a size 10 in my pants.

I believe that when you focus on your health, and reduce your stress levels, it is easy to keep the weight off.

Moreover, when you are healthy, you will have the energy to build your Business.

Today I want to share with you 5 easy ways to take better care of yourself:

1. Get plenty of rest at night. Millionaires do not stay up all night working!
2. Drink plenty of water. I downloaded a water drinking app to help me to stay hydrated. Staying hydrated is good for your organs.
3. Eat plenty of fruits and veggies. Fruits and Vegetables are loaded with phytonutrients which helps the body fight off cancer cells.
4. Exercise 30 minutes a day. This could include walking, jogging, going to the gym, aerobics. Whatever, you choose to do, remember this: Exercise is great for the heart and every time that you exercise, you are making the choice to live healthy.
5. Relax More! Get a monthly massage, carry some lavender oil and do deep breathing daily. I know *firsthand* that stress is bad for the heart!

I hope that you have been inspired to take better care of yourself as you build your business. There is no fun in having Success without your health.

Your Health is Your Wealth!

What do you plan to do to take better care of you?

____

____

____

____

____

____

____

____

____

____

____

____

____

____

____

____

____

____

Conclusion

As I Prepared to write the concluding chapter of this book, I asked myself this question: Did you share everything that you know about Business Growth.

My answer is no, because it would have taken me ten years to write this book. In fact, I believe that I gave you key strategies for building your business by Faith.

Most of all, I believe that the strategies that I have shared in this book is what you need to Build the business of your dreams. Furthermore, I believe that after reading this book, you have what it takes to Grow a Business.

The only thing that is stopping you from growing your business is you. So, get out of your own way, start preparing your mind for business growth, write your vision and get started on that business growth plan.

In conclusion, remember this: when you commit your Business to God, your thoughts will be Established, and God will Direct your path.

Go Grow that Business!

Prayers for Business Growth

Prayer invites the power and the Presence of God in Your Business

A Prayer for Your Mind

Father God,
I ask that you fill my mind with thoughts of peace, Love Joy and abundance. I cast down every thought that hinders my business growth, including thoughts of doubt, lack and fear.

In Jesus name,
Amen

A Prayer for Employees

Father God,
Send me employees with the mindset to work. Cover my employees let their mind be in alignment with my vision and let us walk in agreement. Keep away any employees that come to frustrate my Journey or bring harm to the Business.

In Jesus Name,
Amen

A Prayer for Business Growth

Father God, I thank you for giving me the grace to grow my business. I thank you in advance for prospering and growing my Business. Most of all, I thank you for sending an anointing that will lead to Good success which will result in business growth. Now lord I ask that you strengthen my hands to Build my Business.

In Jesus Name,
Amen

Declarations For

Business Growth

If you decree a thing it shall be established unto you.

I decree and declare:

Today I choose growth over lack.

I have nothing but Good Success. -Joshua 1:6

 I will have an attitude of gratitude, because thanksgiving is my seed for more. – Ephesians 5:20

My God will supply all my needs according to His riches in Glory. -Philippians 4:19

The Lord will increase me and my Children more and more. - Psalms 115:14

I have the mental capacity to handle the growth that God has prepared for me.

I choose Courage over Fear.

I walk by Faith and not in doubt.

About the Author

Shiketa Morgan is a woman of Big Faith, she is married to Charles Morgan, a Mother, a Grandmother, Owner of Learning Days Child Care Centers, Self-Published Author, Blogger and a Business Coach.

Shiketa was born and raised in St. Louis Missouri. On October 5, 2018, she stepped out on Faith and moved to Atlanta, Georgia with her husband

Shiketa's life mission is to inspire others to live and to do business by Faith!

You can find Shiketa Online at:
www.doingbusinessbyfaith.com

Business Growth Journal

Write the Vision and Make it plain

Your Business Growth Thoughts

Your Business Growth Thoughts

Your Business Growth Thoughts

Your Business Growth Thoughts

Your Business Growth Thoughts

Your Business Growth Thoughts

Your Business Growth Thoughts

____

____

____

____

____

____

____

____

____

____

____

____

____

____

____

____

____

____

____

Your Business Growth Thoughts

Your Business Growth Thoughts

Your Business Growth Thoughts

Your Business Growth Thoughts

Your Business Growth Thoughts

Your Business Growth Thoughts

Your Business Growth Thoughts

Your Business Growth Thoughts

Your Business Growth Thoughts

Your Business Growth Thoughts

Your Business Growth Thoughts

Your Business Growth Thoughts

Your Business Growth Thoughts

Your Business Growth Thoughts

Your Business Growth Thoughts

Your Business Growth Thoughts

Your Business Growth Thoughts

Your Business Growth Thoughts

Your Business Growth Thoughts

Your Business Growth Thoughts

Your Business Growth Thoughts

Connect with Shiketa Online

Facebook
http://facebook.com/shiketamorgan
http://facebook.com/doingbusinessbyfaith

Twitter
www.twitter.com/shiketamorgan

Instagram
@shiketamorgan
@doingbusinessbyfaith

Send feedback about this book to:
shiketamo@gmail.com

www.ingramcontent.com/pod-product-compliance
Lightning Source LLC
Chambersburg PA
CBHW031319060726
47590CB00003B/1264